The Ultimate Guide for the Network Marketer's Bride

Get the Love You Desire and Build an Empire

Angela G. Solomon

For my husband Orin, with all of my love, and for our sons, Jacob, Jason, and Jordan. Pursuing your dreams is an ongoing exercise in faith. Never quit.

Published in the United States by
Nine Star Media
1300 Mercantile Lane, Suite 139-DD
Largo, Maryland 20774

Library of Congress Control Number: 2011963245

ISBN: 978-0-984-87021-9

Printed in the United States of America

First Edition

TABLE OF CONTENTS

Chapter 9

FOREWORD

*Y*ou have an amazing opportunity right now. Your partner has joined a network marketing company or is talking about doing so.

You have a big choice as you move through the next few months and years. You can build or you can tear down. You can move closer or you can fly apart.

Yes, you have a choice to make. Luckily, there is help to steer you through the maze in which you've suddenly found yourself. In *The Ultimate Guide for the Network Marketer's Bride*, you'll learn what network marketing actually is, and what it is not. You'll learn what to say when your friends and family protest. And you'll learn what it means to build a business together in a way that builds your relationship and your family while also providing free time, passive income, and perhaps most importantly, hope for the future for you and everyone you care about.

Picture you and your loved one holding hands, turning slowly in a circle, close together. Then your partner starts learning new things, meeting new people, investing time and effort into personal development. He speeds up. This is where the critical choice is. You can speed up right alongside him, staying close, growing together. Or you can stay at the same speed, pulling away from him. Physics doesn't allow you to stay close and go at different speeds. You either move at the same speed, pull apart or actually separate. You have a choice, but you also have tools.

Angela G. Solomon writes from experience as an active mother, smart attorney, supportive wife, and loving partner with her husband Orin in a wildly successful network marketing home-based business. She is a partner in every sense of the word—supporting, building, counseling, and providing a great example of how it's meant to work.

You are critical to the long-term success of the business. Sure, it'll be different and yes, sometimes it will be hard. The good news is you have a resource and you have a support team. Keep *The Ultimate Guide for the Network Marketer's Bride* close. You're not alone!

Diane Kennedy, CPA
The New York Times Bestselling author of
Loopholes of the Rich,
Smart Business, Stupid Business, and others
Baja California, 2011

PRELUDE
10 Things You Will Discover By Reading This Book

1. **How to get more quality time (with his focus 100% on you, without interruptions).**
   You'll learn what to do to make him want to spend more time with you. Plus, when you're together, you'll know how to get all of his attention with no pesky cell phone, text, or business-related interruptions.

2. **What to say to get him to talk about something unrelated to the business.**
   Since your man became involved in network marketing, it seems the business comes up in every conversation. Between his goals, what he has to do, and what his mentor said, you can hardly get a word in edgewise about more important topics—like you, the children, the family, and your relationship. Even when he does try to engage in a "normal" conversation, he always finds a way to relate the topic in some way to the business (and in so doing, piss you off). You'll learn how to say goodbye to attitudes and hello to attention.

3. **How to negotiate family time so you don't feel like he has abandoned his family responsibilities.**

   You have been planning to attend an event for months. You have RSVP'd for two and marked the date on your calendar. You've reminded him often, because you know this network marketing thing has him running around like a crazy man. The evening prior to the event, as you are laying out your clothes with matching accessories to be the best-dressed woman in the place, your man ever-so-delicately informs you that he has a "quick" meeting right before the event, but he'll be home to pick you up in time for you both to go to the event together. The next evening, you find yourself all dressed up with no Prince Charming. You impatiently watch the clock tick away, and with each passing minute, you become more infuriated. This is when you really begin seriously thinking of giving him an ultimatum. How could he not be here as he promised? He knew how important this event was to you. You reminded him about it for a while. You'll discover how to get on his calendar (and stay there!) without fail.

4. **What you should do immediately to make sure all of his time and money is not being spent on a scam.**

   Not all network marketing opportunities are created equally. There are ways to make sure the company is legal and operating with integrity. You may find this to be the most important advice in this book!

5. **Why he is so sold on network marketing (he's a network marketing crazy man!) and what this means for you.**
   Does network marketing make you a little uncomfortable? Are you secretly wondering whether your man has been captured by the Matrix? You'll get some reasonable explanations for the cult-like behavior of your man and his new business associates. It may be contagious.

6. **How to handle women in the business who flirt with your man.**
   Ladies. Pay attention to this. Even if you think your man is immune to advances from other women, let me be the first to clue you in: some woman will want your man. Truth be told, maybe more than one. More importantly, she will not care if he is married or in a relationship. People like to buy things from people who are attractive. It makes sense, then, that there are lots of attractive people in network marketing. A combination of good looks, a great personality, and the ability to speak well can make a person lots of money in this business. It is no secret that your man will be around lots of beautiful women as he attends business-related meetings and conventions. Even the most trusting wife can get a little jealous or suspicious sometimes because the business can easily get a little too "belly-to-belly" for comfort. Whether it is the constant cell phone calls and texts or the more-than-friendly hugs, at some point, you are likely going to suspect foul play—if not on the part of your man, then by some network marketing vixen who is walking that fine line between contacting him for business and reaching

out to him for purely selfish pleasure. Find out what you need to do to force her to pursue an easier target.

7. **What to say to him BEFORE you give him an ultimatum.**
When you get so fed up with him not being home, missing family events, and not spending time with you, you will be tempted to give him an ultimatum. You feel the only way to get his attention (and get him back in your life the way he was before network marketing) is to make him choose: you or this network marketing business. No one appreciates being threatened or bullied. When you approach him from a place of negativity, no one wins. Because even if he does decide to give up the business to make you happy, he will not be happy. He will grow resentful. The effect of your ultimatum and his choice may not be immediately apparent in your relationship, but eventually if he has regrets, you will be blamed. It is better to try to compromise. Can you come up with a solution that will work for both of you? This book will help you find a way for both of you to get what you want. You want love. He wants money. You'll discover some ideas that are sure to make both of you happy.

8. **What to say to him if you've already given him an ultimatum.**
If you have already backed him into a corner (which isn't good) and forced him to choose between you and his network marketing business, don't fret. All may not be lost. All of the other aspects of your relationship being considered, you may be able to implement some of the ideas in this book and have your relationship back on the road to

happiness quicker than you can say "network marketing." Realize though, you may have to work a little harder to show that you are sincerely interested in finding a solution that works for both of you. Your ultimatum revealed a bit of selfishness in you that you will be able to overcome if you say and do the things discussed in this book.

9. **How you can help him make more money, more quickly in network marketing.**
We all know men are fully capable of doing anything they set their minds to do. We also know that with the help of the woman he loves, a man can achieve his goals much faster and a lot easier (isn't this common knowledge?). With your 100% support and belief in him, your man can be *really* successful in network marketing. One of the reasons I wrote this book is to help you see the powerful, positive effect network marketing can have on your family. When you understand this, you and your man can have a meeting of the minds about the business so you both can get what you want from the relationship and the business. A true win-win for everybody. Don't you love it when that happens?

10. **Why network marketing can make your relationship better than it ever was before (hard to believe, I know).**
When you are finished reading this book, you'll understand exactly how to get what you want: lots of love and attention from your man. As an added bonus, you'll get to enjoy all of the gifts he'll shower you with from the money he earns. You'll be one lucky woman. Welcome to your blueprint for love and happiness!

"Men are born to succeed, not to fail."
- Henry David Thoreau

Introduction

*Y*our man comes home excited about a business opportunity. He tries to tell you about it as best he can, but the details are sketchy—what he's saying doesn't make sense. It sounds like a scam. You've heard about these pyramid schemes. You don't want to be a part of it, and you don't want him to be a part of it either. He informs you that it is too late—he's already made the decision to join and has paid the start-up fee. Your initial reaction is anger. How could he make this decision without you? What will be the financial impact of his decision? Will it cost more money (that you may not even have), or did he use money that was designated for another purpose to chase after an empty dream?

A good man makes taking care of his family his priority. This value is often instilled in males during childhood. A man's role as the provider for the family was established centuries ago. In the early days of civilization, men hunted animals to provide food for their families. Our modern-day hunters have traded in their bows and arrows in favor of bow ties or work boots and sheer determination to bring home the proverbial bacon.

Many generations ago, while men were "hunters," women were "gatherers" who concerned themselves with matters closer to home. Fast forward to the 1950s, the popular television show *Leave It To Beaver* depicted the ideal life of women in that era. June Cleaver, the show's matriarch, was a homemaker who served up a hot meal and domestic perfection to her husband when he returned home from work. Whether hunting or working, men were conditioned to be the providers, while women were taught to be the nurturers at home.

Today, gender roles are not as distinctly defined, but societal expectations of men and women remain largely unchanged. Far more women work outside of the home than in the past, with some women holding high-powered, highly paid professional positions. Despite women having more opportunities for financial independence, the weight generally still falls on men to contribute significantly to household income. Similarly, the responsibility for household chores still falls disproportionately on women even when they work outside of the home.

When a woman has a successful career, she commonly seeks a man who earns as much, if not more, than she earns. Men also strive to conform to traditional gender roles. More often than they are willing to admit, men have difficulty being in relationships with women bringing home larger paychecks. Even when a woman works outside of the home, both men and women expect a man to earn his fair share... and then some. To be sure, traditional beliefs about gender roles still prevail.

It is easy to understand why most men continue to feel the pressure of being financial providers. When a family is going through financial challenges like foreclosure or bankruptcy, most people judging the situation will blame the man—he should've gotten a second job or he should've taken the necessary steps to ensure that the family didn't get into a bad situation in the first place. This pressure causes men to think about money constantly. Have you ever heard of a deadbeat mom? Probably not. Deadbeat dads are fathers who do not pay child support. Our society clearly intends for men to continue providing for their families, regardless of whether women are working inside or outside of the home.

Your man views network marketing as a way to become a better provider and improve his family's financial situation. Certainly, there are other reasons people get involved in network marketing. Some want to help others, to give to charity, to have a more flexible schedule, or to work independently without having a boss. But one thing is for sure: at the core of all of these reasons is a necessary prerequisite—money. The primary reason your man got involved in network marketing is that he wants to **Make Lots of Money (MLM)!**

Money is a motivator for many men because having money will allow for a lot of other things: satisfying his obligations as the family's provider, buying more of the things the family *wants* instead of only providing what the family *needs*, spending more time with the family, and working fewer hours so that he can attend family events and spend more time with you. So, you see, he really wants the same things you do. The difference is that by joining a network marketing company, he is focusing on the means to produce the end result.

Who enjoys living paycheck to paycheck with more days left in the month than money? Is it really fun to go places together worrying about your credit card being declined? Are you tired of going without and "making do" instead of getting what you really want? Between you and me, I'm going to let you in on a little secret: your man is tired of living like that, too. He wants a better life for both of you. He is hoping network marketing is the vehicle to get him to financial freedom faster and with more certainty than the forty-year work plan that was commonly followed by previous generations. Not only is the forty-year work plan no longer a viable option, it is virtually non-existent. Job security is rare. Retirement pensions are no longer guaranteed. Social security may be a remnant of the past by the time you need it. Whether through network marketing or some other means, people are wise to rely on entrepreneurial pursuits rather than employment for financial sustainability. As you begin reading this book, my first advice to you is to thank your man. Thank him for having the guts and the vision to try something that is different from what others are doing. Thank him for taking steps toward securing the financial future of his family. Thank him for taking a chance. As the adage says, "If you want something different, you have to do something different." He is not satisfied with the status quo and has decided to take action. Bravo!

While we are in a mood of gratitude, let me extend to you my heartfelt thanks for purchasing my book. Thank you very much!

I'd love it if you could do me a HUGE favor. I'd like to know what you think about this book after you've read it. Please email me your comments.

You can reach me at Angela@mlmwives.com.

Let's get it started!

"There is no security in this life. There is only opportunity."
- Douglas MacArthur

Chapter 1
Is This Network Marketing Thing a Pyramid Scam?

History of Network Marketing

*F*irst things first. Here is the truth about network marketing (also known as multi-level marketing or MLM). Network marketing generates more than $100 billion in revenue per year. The industry attracts people of all backgrounds from all over the world who want to own their own business because of the relatively low start-up costs and relatively high income potential. Network marketing is not a temporary fad, nor is it a new phenomenon. Network marketing in its earliest forms has been around for well over one hundred years. However, it is generally accepted that the first network marketing compensation plan was introduced in 1945. Many people with names you may know—such as Mary Kay Ash, founder of Mary Kay Cosmetics; David McConnell, founder of Avon Products, Inc.; and Earl Tupper, founder of Tupperware—have become extraordinarily wealthy in network marketing. Their businesses, and many others, still offer legitimate, income-earning opportunities today.

A brief study of the history of network marketing begins with merchants in the early 1900s who wanted to sell their products on a larger scale than just their local neighborhood. It was considered a savvy business practice for merchants to employ a sales force to market their wares farther and wider than they could ever reach through their efforts alone. To give the sales force an incentive to sell as much merchandise as possible, the merchants offered the sales force the opportunity to earn money on each unit of product sold, thereby encouraging more sales.

Unlike employee salaries and wages in the traditional workplace, network marketing compensation plans are structured to pay very fairly. Those who sell the most get paid the most. Network marketing companies reward production. On a regular job, whether you are a slacker or a gunner, when you share the same job title or job grade with someone else, both of your paychecks are virtually the same. If you are fortunate to have a job that does so, you could be rewarded with bonuses around the holidays for personally performing over and above employer expectations.

Network marketing, however, is structured to reward those who go the extra mile for themselves and who train others to do the same. Without a doubt, network marketing offers a much more cooperative working atmosphere than the corporate environment. In the traditional workplace, if you train someone to do your job, and they learn to do it as well or better than you, you'll soon be replaced by your trainee. Conversely, it is a network marketer's dream to introduce someone to the business who can outwork him. The philosophy of network marketing is very different from the "every man for himself" philosophy to which you may be accustomed, so don't be surprised if it takes some time to adjust your mindset to the concept of cooperative marketing.

Now that you have examples of names and companies you know that were built with a network marketing structure and you have an understanding of how the network marketing industry began, let's address the BIG concern most people have who question the validity of the network marketing industry: Is it a pyramid? Below is a statement made in 1998 by Debra A. Valentine, who was the General Counsel for the United States Federal Trade Commission:

> "Some people confuse pyramid and Ponzi schemes with legitimate multilevel marketing. Multilevel marketing programs are known as MLM's, and unlike pyramid or Ponzi schemes, MLM's have a real product to sell. More importantly, MLM's actually sell their product to members of the general public, without requiring these consumers to pay anything extra or to join the network marketing system. MLM's may pay commission to a long string of distributors, but these commissions are paid for real retail sales..."[1]

Ms. Valentine's statement on "pyramid schemes" can be found in its entirety on my website, www.mlmwives.com/

---

1 Excerpt from the Prepared Statement of Debra A. Valentine, General Counsel for the U.S. Federal Trade Commission, presented at the International Monetary Fund's Seminar on Current Legal Issues Affecting Central Banks, Washington, DC, May 13, 1998, United States Federal Trade Commission, www.ftc.gov.

Guide. As Ms. Valentine's quote indicates, pyramid schemes do exist, but so does legitimate multi-level (network) marketing. Individuals who have operated fraudulent schemes and duped consumers out of money have tainted some people's perception of the network marketing industry. The truth is that network marketing is a lucrative industry in which many legitimate and profitable businesses operate.

As with any business opportunity, it is important to do your due diligence. Check out the company's website and talk to people who are currently involved with the company. If possible, try to reach out to at least one person who has been with the company for a relatively long time. They can give you a historical perspective on the company and may also inspire you with details of why they have remained loyal to the company and what they have done to be successful. You never know—through your research, you may find that you have inadvertently recruited a business mentor!

In today's technological age, the first place we go to research anybody or anything is an Internet search engine. A word of caution about the information you will see on the Internet: Don't believe everything you read! There will always be disgruntled individuals who use the Internet as a forum to slam a company they feel failed them for whatever reason. The bigger the company, the more bad reviews you are bound to find in your Google search.

Fortunately, more credible information can be obtained from independent sources. You can put your fears about network marketing to rest by contacting your state's consumer protection agency, the local Better Business Bureau, and the Direct Selling Association to inquire about any network marketing company. Your state's consumer protection agency and your local Better Business Bureau will have information about complaints filed by residents of your state against various companies. You can also check with the consumer protection agency and Better Business Bureau of the state in which the company's home office is located for information about complaints and compliance.

The company you are inquiring about may have no record of any complaints being filed against it. That is reassuring. However, even if you find there have been complaints lodged against the company you are investigating, don't stop your research and draw any hasty conclusions. Anyone can file a complaint about a company for any reason, so it is important to dig further to find out more information about the complaint and how it was resolved. As you know, disgruntled people can be spiteful enough to file baseless complaints in an attempt to damage a company's reputation. Often, such erroneous complaints are quickly dismissed with a valid explanation.

While you are on the Internet, check out the Direct Selling Association (www.dsa.org). Founded in 1910, the DSA offers membership to companies exhibiting the highest possible business ethics. If the company you are inquiring about is a member of the DSA, you can trust that the company is legitimate. If the company you are inquiring about is not a member, it does not necessarily mean the company is a scam. Definitely continue your research and consider encouraging the company to apply for membership. Membership in the DSA will give the company's sales force and the general public further assurance of the company's ethical business practices.

They're In On It, Too?

Warren Buffett is arguably America's most-admired and most-followed investor. He is consistently named as one of the world's richest people. Buffett is the largest shareholder and the Chief Executive Officer of the very highly regarded Berkshire Hathaway. Under Buffett's leadership, Berkshire Hathaway purchased a network marketing company in 2002. Buffet considers that acquisition one of his best-ever investments.[2]

Both Donald J. Trump and Robert T. Kiyosaki are known for their success in business. Donald J. Trump is a world-renowned businessman, a best-selling author, and the executive producer of the top-rated television reality shows, *"The Apprentice"* and *"The Celebrity Apprentice."* Robert T. Kiyosaki is an investor, businessman, and best-selling author. His book, *Rich Dad, Poor Dad*, is the longest-running best seller on *The New York Times*, *The Wall Street Journal*, *USA Today*, and *Business Week* best-seller lists.

Both Trump and Kiyosaki recommend network marketing in the book they co-authored, *Why We Want You To Be Rich*.[3] In the book, Kiyosaki says network marketing is an industry for people who want to change their lives and get the necessary skills and attitude training to be successful business owners. Taking Kiyosaki's recommendation a step further, Trump states, "Network marketing has proven itself to be a viable and rewarding source of income...There have been some re-

---

2 "Move Over, Mary Kay", Inc.com, © 2010 Mansueto Ventures LLC, http://www.inc.com/ss/new-guard-direct-selling#0.
3 Donald J. Trump and Robert T. Kiyosaki, *Why We Want You To Be Rich* (Rich Press, 2006), 305-312.

markable examples of success, and those successes have been earned through diligence, enthusiasm and the right product combined with timing."

Robert G. Allen, best-selling author of the hugely popular book for entrepreneurs, *Multiple Streams of Income*, views network marketing as a way to create a valuable stream of residual income that flows into your life 24 hours a day— even when you sleep. In his special report entitled, "Creating Wealth the Enlightened Way," Allen writes this about network marketing: "...my experience has been fantastic! Once the income starts to flow, it's like an oil well in your back yard. It just keeps pumping out profits. Looking back, I wonder how I could have overlooked such a powerful moneymaking idea for so many years. And I'm saddened because those same misconceptions are holding back so many other smart people."[4]

If successful businessmen like Warren Buffett, Donald Trump, Robert Kiyosaki, and Robert Allen all believe network marketing is an excellent vehicle for generating wealth, I'm convinced. Are you? Obviously, network marketing is not for everyone. Everyone who joins a network marketing company is not going to become wealthy, much like everyone who goes to school will not make the honor roll. Everyone has different skills and strengths. If your man has the desire, drive, and determination to build a network marketing business, support him. He may be (or can learn to be) the above-average person who earns an above-average income to provide you with the above-average lifestyle of your dreams!

---

4 Robert G. Allen, "Creating Wealth the Enlightened Way", 2002, www.theenlightenedway.com.

"If your mind isn't open, keep your mouth shut too."
- Sue Grafton

Chapter 2

Honey, Did I Mention We're In Business?

*G*reat! You've read this far, which hopefully means you will be open to the ideas and solutions I will be sharing with you in this book.

Maybe your man consulted you about joining a network marketing business prior to paying the start-up fee, or maybe he didn't. Either way, if he is in, you are in, too. Obviously, you would feel better about the business if you agreed to his decision prior to him paying the money. Whether you were on board or not, your support can make the difference between his success and his failure in the business.

To increase your comfort level and knowledge about the business, make an effort to learn as much as you can about the company. Go to the company's website. Go to where other representatives of the company are. This includes meetings, teleconferences, and Internet forums. Watch the company's DVD and read through the marketing material that convinced your man the opportunity was for him. In addition to all of the above, start finding answers to the following questions:

- What is the vision and mission of the network marketing company for which your man is marketing?
- What are the company's revenues? How long has it been in business? Is the company growing?
- Is there a steady or increasing demand for the product or service being sold?
- Who owns the company?
- Who are the company's competitors?
- Who runs the company?
- Does the company have a reputation of integrity?
- How does the company train its representatives on the products or services offered?
- What type of sales training do representatives receive?
- Is the company's product or service something your man can sell enthusiastically?
- What is the average time a representative remains active with the company?
- Is the company a member of the Direct Selling Association?

Answering these questions is the best way to mind *your* business. You want to make sure that the business is built on a solid foundation, instead of wasting valuable time building a house of cards that could fall at any moment. Network marketing takes too much valuable time, energy, and sacrifice to get involved with just any company. Do your research to make sure the company will be around for the long haul. Nothing is guaranteed, but you can do your due diligence and increase your probability of longevity with the company.

As I mentioned in Chapter 1, remember to check with the Better Business Bureau (BBB) locally and the BBB in the state where the company is headquartered. Check also with your state's consumer protection office to make sure the network marketing company you are involved with is a legitimate network marketing business opportunity. When you have completed your due diligence and you feel assured the company offers a viable opportunity with profit potential, take a deep breath and get ready. It's on!

Now, it is time to examine your family's vision and goals as they relate to the business. It is really helpful to go through this exercise with your man. Talking this through with him will let him know he has your support in this business venture. I recommend you take out a piece of paper and pen to write down the answers to the following questions.

What is your WHY for getting involved in network marketing? Your WHY should make you cry. I'm not kidding. It should be so compelling that the thought of it makes you weep. It must be bigger than you. You may say, "I want to make a lot of money." But there are a lot of people who want to make a lot of money who remain broke year after year. WHY do you want to make a lot of money? What will you do with it? Will you fund your child's private school or college tuition, retire your parents or buy them a new home, help your church or charity meet a fundraising goal, or pay all of your bills so you can spend your time volunteering for a cause dear to your heart? Strangely enough, we will let ourselves down more often than we will disappoint others. Having a WHY or a goal bigger than yourself will keep you focused when the going gets tough—and I can guarantee that you will face challenges! Your WHY will keep you going when you are tempted to quit.

As an example of a compelling WHY, I recently heard National Football League (NFL) superstar Deion Sanders give a powerful, tear-jerking speech at his induction into the NFL Hall of Fame. He told the story of his mother who worked in a hospital pushing a cleaning cart. His mother worked very hard to provide for Deion and his sister as a single parent, and made sure her children had all they needed and most of what they desired. In spite of his mother's efforts, Deion was ashamed of her because he was teased by other children about his mother's occupation. While Deion was still a young boy, he vowed to himself that he was going to make a lot of money one day so his mother would never have to push the hospital cart another day of her life.

As this real life story illustrates, Deion's WHY was bigger than himself. It even made him cry as he delivered his speech that day. He strived to achieve his goals for the benefit of someone other than himself—his mother. When he encountered obstacles along the way, Deion told the audience he thought of his mother pushing the cart, and that thought pushed him through. Deion's WHY made him cry. It motivated him to reach his goal regardless of the challenges he faced. With his mother sitting in the front row to hear, Deion told the audience that he has paid all of his mother's bills since 1989, clearly implying that he in fact achieved his goal of retiring his mother from her job at the hospital.

Make sure your WHY is as compelling and motivating as Deion's, and your determination to be successful will propel you to the top. I recommend you write down your WHY and your goals and put them in a place where you can be reminded of them often. You and your man can share the same WHY or each of you can have your own WHY. Some people put their WHY on the refrigerator, while others put it on the bathroom mirror. If you spend a lot of time driving, you may want to keep your WHY in a visible location in your car. You should read your WHY statement at least twice a day: once in the morning and once before you go to bed. Keeping your WHY in your thoughts will help keep you focused on achieving your goals. This constant reminder will keep you motivated on those not-so-great days, when you are feeling doubtful and discouraged. Even on the super days, when all seems to be going your way, look at your reason WHY you are doing your business and you will be even more energized to reach your goals faster.

Whether you decide to actively work the network marketing business with your man or you decide to support his efforts with your encouragement, you should both be in agreement with regard to your family's goals—your collective dreams, wants and desires. To supercharge your motivation, I recommend you create a visual representation of your family's goals. You may have heard of a *"vision board."* A vision board is created by going through books, magazines, the Internet, and even your own personal photo collection, cutting out pictures and attaching them to a standard-sized poster board you can get from any office supply store. Along with pictures, you can cut out letters to spell words on your vision board, and you can even make designs by hand to decorate the board. The idea is that a picture is worth a thousand words. Your vision board of your family's goals will help keep you focused.

Similar to your written WHY statement, your vision board should be placed in a prominent place where you will have a constant reminder of why you are committed to having success in the business. When you are committed to success, failure is not an option. Working with your man on a written WHY statement and a vision board will strengthen your relationship and your business.

To make implementing your success plan easier, I have created a Mobile Mission Statement™ (MMS) for you. The MMS is where you write down your WHY, your goals, and your action plan to achieve your goals. Keep your MMS in your purse and give a copy to your man for him to keep in his wallet. You will see your MMS often and stay focused on your plans for success.

Mobile Mission Statement

My WHY	My Action Plan
(Use this space to write or paste pictures to represent your WHY)	What steps will you take to achieve each of your long-term goals?

	1. Long-term goal #1
	   a.
	
	   b.

	2. Long-term goal #2
	   a.
	
	   b.

My Long-term Goals 1. 2. 3.	Notes & Great Quotes

You can download your copy of the Mobile Mission Statement™ and find out more information about creating a vision board on my website at www.mlmwives.com/Guide.

The next question you should ask yourself is, "Am I ready to embrace change and experience personal growth?" Network marketing teaches you so much about yourself and about other people. Your outlook on life will change. Your circle of friends will change. Your attitude will change. For most people, all of these changes will be for the better.

The first place change will begin to occur will be in your mindset—your outlook on life. If you have not had any business owners in your life up until this point, you may not understand the time it takes to operate a business. The mindset of an employee is very different from the mindset of a business owner. Employees work their eight hours, come home, and get ready to do another eight hours the next day. Employees tolerate Monday through Friday to enjoy their weekly "vacation" days—Saturday and Sunday. Employees work just hard enough to keep their jobs, and will do even less if they know they can get away with it.

Owning a business requires significantly more time and effort than a job does. Business owners work "eight 'til faint." There is no steady guaranteed pay check. Business owners create their own income by selling their products or services. Thus, the more business owners work, the more they get paid. Conversely, no work equals no pay. Business owners are motivated to work as much as they can to make as much money as they can. Weekdays, weekends, late nights—it doesn't matter. They do whatever it takes to keep their businesses thriving.

Business owners can't be lazy and shirk work because they would only be cheating themselves.

Until the contrast between an employee mindset and a business owner mindset is completely understood, you may not have much patience for the time your man wants to devote to his business. You may not fully grasp the commitment that has to be made for him to realize his long-term vision for the business. You may not understand the sacrifice it takes to be successful in network marketing. You may not know that you don't know all of this because most of the people you know put in their forty hours and relax over the weekend.

Through business ownership, you will grow a lot, learn a lot, and hopefully earn a lot as well. Network marketing has been affectionately called a "personal growth program with a compensation plan attached." You will begin to understand that the business takes a lot of time to build. You will also realize it is better to put in the work now to be able to truly enjoy life a lot sooner and a lot better. If you are shown an alternative, would you choose to work hard for the next forty years with only two weeks of vacation each year? If you have to work hard anyway, why not work hard for yourself? Hopefully, after answering all of the questions presented above, you'll be ready to give your man the space he needs to soar.

"Confidence is contagious. So is lack of confidence."
- Michael O'Brien

Chapter 3

Payback is a Mother

*O*nce you verify your network marketing company is not a scam and have decided, with your man, WHY you (collectively) are involved in the business, you can focus on the most important task at hand: helping your man get back his initial investment in the business. Getting the first paycheck from the business will increase your confidence level in the business (Hey, this thing really works!) and will also reduce some of your financial risk. When you earn the investment back, you will be poised for profit mode—an ideal place to be in any business.

The key to recouping the initial investment into a network marketing company is to understand the company's compensation plan. The compensation plan details exactly what independent business owners must do to earn a commission check from the company. In a product-based business, you may have to sell a specific number of products. In a service-based business, you may have to enroll a certain number of customers. When you understand exactly what you need to do to make money, you can make sure you and your man take action every day, without fail, to move the business forward.

A key characteristic of network marketing that makes it so attractive is that you can earn money not only from what you do personally, but also from the efforts of others you recruit into your business. It is imperative that you figure out how to generate this passive income as outlined in your company's compensation plan. After you determine exactly what you need to do to generate passive income that will be paid to you in the form of commission checks, you can set some business goals. Grab your man. This is another exercise you should do together that will make getting his time, love, and attention much easier in the days to come.

Setting business goals is important because you must have an idea of where you want to go before you can actually get there. Many people have good intentions, but without a clear vision of your goals, you may not take the proper steps to grow your business. Let me give you a hypothetical example. The company's compensation plan indicates that commission will be earned when you sponsor a new person into the business and that new person sells a product. In your "business newbie" excitement, you go out and speak so passionately about the lucrative opportunity your business offers that you get ten people to sign up into your business. Pleased with yourself, you pat yourself on the back and eagerly await your commission check from the company with much anticipation. Is your check coming or are you waiting on disappointment? I am sure you realized that the company in this example required two actions to get paid: sponsoring a new person *and* that new person selling a product. You were very diligent in your sponsoring. However, because you lacked a complete understanding of the compensation plan, the people you sponsored did not make any product sales. The requirements of the compensation plan were not met, and as a result, no commission was earned.

If this happens to you or your man, you'll be devastated. You'll feel you've done all of this work, but the company has failed you because you did not get paid when you signed up ten new people into the business. Your confidence will diminish and the ten people you sponsored based on your excitement about the opportunity will follow you, their leader, into despair and doubt about their decision to join the company. This is why understanding the compensation plan and business goal setting go hand-in-hand. Taking action aimlessly or without a complete and thorough understanding of how you make money will result in disappointment.

Understanding the compensation plan is important. Setting goals based on the compensation plan is even more important. Working toward a goal that maximizes income based on the requirements of the compensation plan is vital. You and your man should consistently set profit targets as you grow your business.

Here's a great story. Ted and Alexis, a newlywed couple, joined a network marketing company. Well, the real story is that Ted joined the company and told Alexis about it later. The couple purchased a home with an adjustable mortgage, and the monthly house payment was increasing every month. Unfortunately, their income was staying the same, so they were feeling the financial crunch. Their bills were causing too much stress in their lives, and more specifically in their new marriage. They initially considered trying to get a loan. They thought if they could get some temporary relief from their bills, they would feel a lot better and be able get back on track financially. Being the smart young couple that they are, they quickly realized that a loan would only be a short-term solution. In the long run, they would be back in the same place—or worse—because a loan has to be paid back.

That's when Ted took action. He found a network marketing company with a product he could be passionate about and a compensation plan he understood. Ted was a teacher by trade, so he already had the skills to teach and train people. To him, network marketing would be better than any loan because the profits would increase his income, there was no limit to the amount of commission he could earn, and the money earned would not have to be paid back to anyone. Ted was sold.

His wife wasn't. Alexis knew they needed extra money, but she was concerned about the time a business like this would take. After all, they were newlyweds, and she enjoyed spending time doing things after work and on weekends with her husband. She felt that she was already sacrificing enough couple time for his outside commitments. In addition to his teaching job, Ted was also a high school football coach. Coaching required a huge time commitment in the evenings and on weekends during the fall months. Adding to that, Ted had many friends from high school and college who regularly invited him to social gatherings, and Ted felt a friendly obligation to attend.

Ted started his business in the spring, but Alexis already had an eye on the future. She told him that in the fall, he would have to choose between coaching football and working the network marketing business; otherwise, she would never see him, which would not be good for their new marriage.

Ted knew he would have to make some great things happen to convince his wife that he could handle all of his obligations and spend time with her, too. His desire to make extra money was to help ease their financial strain and make room in their budget for starting a family. Anticipating the cost of diapers, food, and day care, he knew that their income had to increase to make everything work financially. Talk about a WHY. Wow!

Ted also wanted to make his wife happy and spend time with her. His plan was to use his days during the summer months when school was out to work hard on his business. Alexis would be at work during the day, so there would be very little change in their time spent together.

Ted had a passion for coaching football. He enjoyed helping the players grow and develop in the game and in their lives. Because he played football himself throughout his childhood and in college, it was a joy for him to coach. He did not want to argue with his wife, but he had no plans to give up coaching football anytime soon. Before he started teaching full-time when school resumed in September, Ted wanted to show Alexis that the business could really be the answer to their prayers.

This young, intelligent husband knew money would make his honey happy. Ted knew he had to get his money right to get Alexis's attitude right. With his WHY in mind and his goals set, Ted earned a commission check at the end of the summer that was 15 times more than the first commission check he'd earned when he started his business back in the spring. Cha-ching! Instead of pinching pennies, he took his wife out to splurge on a nice dinner with some of his earnings. She was impressed and urged him to continue building the business through the fall months of football season. She was sold! With Ted and Alexis on the same page about the business, the sky was the limit for them.

Set short term, achievable business goals to allow for some quick success to keep you motivated in the business. Duplicate this goal setting system over and over again, measuring your results along the way and adjusting your efforts as you find out what works and what doesn't work. Understanding the compensation plan, setting business goals, and working to achieve those goals will have you well on your way to earning the initial investment back. This puts you on the path to even greater profits. Payback of your business start-up fee is the mother of future success!

"Few things can help an individual more than to place responsibility on him, and to let him know that you trust him."
- Booker T. Washington

Chapter 4

Show Me the Money...Or Else!

*T*ime has passed and you haven't seen any real results. He has been spending a lot of time on the computer, at meetings, or on the telephone (or all three). Even when he's at home, he is talking about how your lives are going to change when the business takes off. He's making big promises, but small money. Not a good combination from a woman's perspective.

Money, or the lack thereof, can be the source of huge conflicts in relationships. Problems with finances can cause even the most supportive woman to lose faith. Compound financial difficulties with the emotional disconnection you feel because his free time is largely spent working on his business instead of with you, and you can quickly become impatient with your man and his new business venture.

To relieve some of the financial pressure, it is important that you and your man keep your current sources of income flowing until you are making steady, consistent income from the network marketing business. If the network marketing business is your man's full-time gig, you would be wise to maintain your steady income from your job, while your man builds the network marketing business. Many successful network marketers are able to retire from their jobs and have their wives quit their jobs to be stay-at-home mothers to their children. But, timing is everything. Quitting jobs and burning career bridges too early can be detrimental to your family's financial situation. Network marketing commissions can be inconsistent in the early stages of the business while living expenses are steadily increasing.

If your man has not resigned from his employment, try to maintain your family's lifestyle solely on your steady W-2 income plus the income he is making from the business. Consider depositing his entire paycheck from his job into a savings account where it can be easily accessed if necessary. Attempting to live without withdrawing any money from the savings account will help you decide when it is financially feasible for him to quit his job and work on the business full-time. If after six months, your family is living comfortably on your paycheck and his business earnings, your man may want to consider his career options. If he is serious about taking his business to the next level, and he has a six-month salary cushion saved in the bank, he may decide to take the entrepreneurial leap of faith and quit his job.

If your man decides to leave his job, the loss of his guaranteed income will create financial uncertainty, which may be scary for you at times. As employees, you both knew exactly how much money you would receive each month to cover bills and other living expenses. When your man is earning commission, your monthly income will fluctuate. Commission is based on sales, and sales vary depending on numerous factors. He could have a super month of record sales, or he could have a slow month with less than stellar sales.

The variability in his income may cause you to be uneasy. Do not allow your fear to sabotage his efforts. Think about the money in the savings account and take comfort in knowing that, if necessary, you can easily access the money you need to make ends meet.

Everyone has ups and downs in business. One month of sales that do not meet expectations should not cause financial ruin. Two months of lagging sales and low commission requires a visit to the business goals and action plan you created based on the compensation plan. A review of the company's sales training tapes will also be helpful to generate ideas about how to increase the success rate of closing new prospects and customers. If month three ends with lower business income than month two, your man may need to start looking for part-time or full-time employment to keep the household financially stable.

I cannot stress enough the importance of maintaining steady employment income until the business commissions are consistent. Quitting jobs prematurely will cause financial strain and emotional distress that will negatively impact progress in the business. Customers and prospects will be repelled by the desperation you will unconsciously exude. When people feel your urgent need for the sale, they don't respond favorably. Working a network marketing business under financial pressure can be like a hamster running on a wheel—working hard and not getting very far. Be smart. Jobs should not be terminated to impress others or to see *if* you will be successful in the business. Jobs should be terminated only after consistent, proven success with the business. After this lengthy lecture about uncertainty, commissions, and success, you already know that until the money he generates from his network marketing business matches or replaces your income on a consistent basis, you should definitely keep your job.

As tempting as it may be, try to refrain from complaining about the amount of time your man is putting toward the business and the lack of results he has to show for it. Network marketing is not a "get rich quick" business. It is a business that is built slowly and steadily, one person and one sale at a time. You and your man must commit for the long haul. Patience is key. As the saying goes, "Rome was not built in a day." Neither is a network marketing business. Network marketing is a numbers game, and it takes time to go through the numbers. Lots of *no's* and enough *yes's* can lead you to a lot of success. Perseverance will determine your destiny. You have to stay in the game to be a winner.

If the money is not coming into your household as fast as you would like, review your WHY and your family's goals together. Set new short-term business goals and establish a new action plan together to achieve some quick and easy success. Review the compensation plan again. Are there opportunities to earn income that you may have overlooked or possibly did not understand when you were getting started in the business?

Pump up your own personal motivation by listening to a company conference call or attending a meeting or a conference. Buy a few personal development books, audio books, or CDs featuring uplifting, motivational speakers like Anthony Robbins, Darren Hardy, Zig Ziglar, or Jim Rohn. Read the books and listen to the CDs yourself and share them with your man. Audio books are very convenient because you can download them on your MP3 player. CDs are great, too, because you can listen to them in your car while you are driving to work or running errands.

Before blasting his dreams or drowning him in negativity and ultimatums, STOP and THINK. Your criticism will actually have the effect of crushing his confidence and slowing down the pace of his success (which is the opposite of what you want). Remember the biblical principle, "Do unto others as you would have them do unto you." Surely you would want him to support you in your personal and business endeavors, so give your man the same consideration. Think of the lifestyle you both can have if this business really works. Have some compassion for the man who loves you so much that he doesn't mind working hard to provide a better lifestyle for you.

If you are having trouble with your long-term vision for the network marketing business, stay in the short-term realm. Re-commit yourself and your support of your man for just one more week. Set a business goal for the week together and measure the results. What worked? What didn't? Do more of what worked. Stop doing what didn't. Write this motto down and remember it: "Week to week. Support and repeat." Network marketing is simple, but it is not easy. With your unconditional support, it will be easier for your man to stay the course to success.

If your man stays focused and puts forth effort every day toward the results the compensation plan rewards, he will eventually have lots of success and make lots of money. This will be awesome and very rewarding, emotionally and financially. He will be proud. You will be prouder—and happier, too.

Enjoy the good times. Like big corporations and other small businesses, network marketing is subject to ups and downs based on the state of the economy. It can be like a roller coaster—thrilling at the top and scary on the descent. This is typical of most businesses and not unique to the network marketing industry. It can be a cyclical business. Sometimes, you may have to do what you have to do to keep your financial situation afloat. If you enjoyed the benefits of the good times, be prepared to make some sacrifices in the bad times until the good times come around again. What does this mean? If your man's success in network marketing allowed you to quit your job, but now sales are slow and money is tight, you should consider getting a job (even if you were able to quit previously) or finding other ways to bring income into the household until business improves for him. It is important to be supportive of him during difficult financial times. Don't start blaming, nagging, and smothering him in negativity. He will already be feeling worse than your words could ever make him feel if it comes to this point. Don't kick your man when he's down. It makes it harder for him to get back up.

Of course, I have a true story to illustrate this. Brendon, a full-time entrepreneur and his wife Katrina, a financial analyst, were having some success in their network marketing business. The commission checks were increasing every week and life was good. Because of the money they were making from the business, they agreed that Katrina should quit her job and be a stay-at-home mother to their one-year-old son. Katrina gave her boss the required two weeks' notice and happily said goodbye to her work outside of the home.

All went well for about three years. Due to the declining economy and the tight job market in their local area, customers were not buying as many of their products. Brendon and Katrina's business suffered. Before their savings were completely depleted, Katrina decided that she should go back to work. She made this suggestion to Brendon, who felt awful about it, but he knew that it was the right thing to do for their family.

So, Brendon and Katrina had to make some adjustments, but their long-term goal to be financially free remained unchanged. They relocated to an area less affected by the downturn of the national economy where more employment opportunities were available. While Katrina worked during the day, Brendon stayed home with their son to save on day care costs. Brendon concentrated on building his business in the evenings when Katrina returned home from work. Despite the challenges, instead of quitting, they remained committed to each other and their business. Brendon is now positioned for a promotion to an income level that will allow Katrina to once again be at home full-time with their son.

Brendon and Katrina are excellent examples of standing together through tough times. Life was challenging and Katrina may have had her doubts, but she did what was necessary to allow Brendon to work through the business challenges. They were able to turn their business around and are stronger financially and romantically than they ever were in the past. I've heard it said that you can't have a testimony without a test. Brendon and Katrina were tested and stayed true to their pursuit of their goals and dreams as a couple.

Just like Katrina, you should enjoy the bounty of the good times. When times aren't going as well, stand by your man wholeheartedly. If you can enjoy the sunshine, you should be able to withstand the rain. The more supportive you are, the faster you both will be on the upside of the rollercoaster again.

"When you work hard, you can play hard." - My Dad

Chapter 5

Gimme A...

*a*s you have been reading this book so far, you have un-doubtedly said to yourself, "What's in it for me? I thought this book was about getting the love I desire. All I've been reading about is what I need to do to help him in his network marketing business."

Well, now is the perfect time for me to clear out the trees so that you can see the forest.

Are you familiar with the Law of Reciprocity? It is a well-known principle of generosity that generally means "give and you shall receive." It is a law of cause and effect. The Law of Reciprocity says what you give is what you get back in return.

There are two important exceptions to this rule that you should know:

1. If you do something for someone else with the inten-tion of getting something in return, the law will not apply.

2. You may not receive from the person to whom you gave. Your bounty may come to you from other people, in other ways.

But, in most cases, when you give from your heart without expectation of receiving anything back, the person who receives will appreciate your kindness and return the favor. Your return may not be in the same form as what you gave, but it will be a return nonetheless.

Let's bring the concept of the Law of Reciprocity to your current situation as the supportive partner of a man diligently working to build his network marketing business. Up until this point in the book, I have advised you on ways to help your man succeed in his business. Hopefully, you've helped him get his initial investment back, helped him generate some additional commissions, and even held your tongue when his work in the business has taken more of his time than you would have preferred. If you have done this, with the pure motive of wanting to see him reach his goals or with the genuine belief that network marketing can change both of your lives, he will feel in his heart that you support him 100%. He will know you have his back. This "you and me against the world" feeling is priceless. With you by his side, he will feel he can conquer any challenge the world presents. Knowing there is someone to depend on in good times and in bad times is as important to men as it is to us. When he knows you support him unconditionally, he will be unstoppable.

It is very difficult to build a network marketing business without the support of your significant other. When your man hears stories from other men in the business who have wives or girlfriends who complain and pile on the guilt for spending time away from the family (they obviously need a copy of this book ASAP!), he will be extremely thankful that you are by his side and will want to reward you for your loyal support.

If I haven't said it enough, let me say it once again: Building a network marketing business is hard work. Network marketing is simple, but it is not easy. I believe when you work hard, you should play hard. (That's what my dad always said!) So when those commissions start rolling in, *celebrate success!*

I can tell you from my own personal experience being around successful network marketers that network marketing can truly make dreams come true. I personally know several people who retired their parents from their jobs, bought their parents houses, and purchased custom-built dream homes for themselves. I know a guy who travels via private jet to his out-of-state meetings and yet another woman who has a new diamond ring so spectacular that it puts the "ING" in BLING! Talk about an upgrade! I also know a family who traveled around the world for an entire year enjoying time together and visiting places many people will never see because of the residual income they earn from their network marketing business. I don't even have to tell you about all of the designer shoes and tailored clothes network marketers wear. I'm sure you've already heard. Stories of people paying cash for fancy exotic cars and donating more than they could have ever dreamed to churches and charities are also very common.

The reason I mention this to you is to highlight real examples of the benefits that success in network marketing can provide. It can be a powerful way to generate the wealth you need to live your dreams. If you stay committed and never quit, you are bound to earn enough money to begin experiencing life in ways you never thought were possible. The extra money may initially serve as a helpful supplement to your family's income. But, with a strong and focused work ethic, you and your man may eventually be able to live more than comfortably on your network marketing income alone. It is my hope that by reading this book, you will understand how critical your support is to the level of income your man earns in network marketing.

The money your man has earned (with your support, of course) may not be enough to buy a Lamborghini or to cover the cost of a new building for your church. Nonetheless, it is more than you would have had if he were not building the business. He earned it. And you did, too. Reward yourselves!

Refer back to your Mobile Mission Statement™, your WHY and your vision board. Are there any of your dreams, wants or desires that can be satisfied now? You've been sacrificing quality time and being understanding and generous with your help and support, so now it's "gimme time"—time for you to reap some rewards. Maybe it's splurging on a designer purse, an expensive piece of jewelry, a pair of shoes you've always dreamed about, an exotic vacation, a gift you've always wanted to give someone else, or a trip to visit family members you haven't seen for a while. Whatever it is, you absolutely MUST do something to reward yourself. Treating yourself will make you feel like a million bucks, and it will also give you the willpower to keep doing what you are doing to have even more success.

Material things are nice, but honestly, the best things in life do not have a price tag. There are intangible benefits to be realized from success in network marketing that are worthy of mentioning here. One of the most important benefits of network marketing success is a close, loving relationship. You know the camaraderie and closeness that strangers who come together to play on a team have when they are striving to win games together? They develop a familial "all for one and one for all" mindset, and are willing to give their all for each other in the quest for a championship. Much like teammates, but far more intimate and thereby more intense, is a couple working together on something in which they both believe. They weather the storms together and toast to the good times together. Come what may, it doesn't matter, as long as they have each other. They are operating on one accord. This unbreakable bond can be yours when you both endure the sacrifices and enjoy the rewards of network marketing together.

When your man joins a network marketing company, you have no idea how successful he will be. You have no way of knowing whether it will work and how it will be incorporated into your lives with all of the other commitments you have vying for your time. It will be tough at first. There will be lots of work, but little return on time invested. He will be tempted to quit. You will be tempted to make him quit. There will be a car on the emotional rollercoaster of network marketing with your names engraved on it. In short, it will be quite a ride.

Fast forward twelve, twenty-four, or heck, sixty months. Again, network marketing takes time and is not a get rich quick vehicle. Regardless of how long it takes, what if you and your man build a solid business with a huge downline of team members who are as passionate about their businesses as you are about yours? What if you and your man reach the top position in the marketing plan and are generating more income from your business than you ever thought possible? What if you awaken every day grateful for your man and your network marketing business, both of which have been such a blessing to you and so many others? What if you are no longer ashamed of your "MLM thing," and people who previously spoke negatively about your business are now genuinely interested because they've witnessed your success? There is a satisfaction that comes from working hard, doing it well, and being recognized by all of your peers for your achievements. The feeling is intensely exciting, emotional, and affirming all at once. When your man experiences this feeling, he'll know that the sacrifices he made for success were worth it. The cost of the initial investment to join the network marketing company? $$$ Having a man whose accomplishments are admired by many, but whose heart belongs to only you? Priceless.

By all means, enjoy all of the fruits of your combined labor. Accept accolades and compliments from others graciously, boast about your man's greatness with tactful humility, and of course, hit the shopping mall if that is what you enjoy. When your man asks you what you want because he wants to spoil you for being everything to him, don't be shy! Speak up and claim your goodies! Whenever you get frustrated with the business and feel lonely because your man is away working the business, you can think of all that you have gained, tangible and intangible, from his work in the business. Thinking this way will keep you going. At least for one more week. Remember our motto: "Week to week. Support and repeat!"

The Law of Reciprocity has two parts: giving and receiving. So does the Law of Gimme (okay, it's not really an official law, but work with me, girlfriend!). It is fine, wonderful, dandy, and great to be able to celebrate success one time. I don't know about you, but if you are anything like me, you can almost never get too much of a good thing. Receiving gifts is most certainly a good thing. Being able to be a blessing to other people is tremendous as well. Celebrating success is most definitely an awesome feeling. So, let's make sure we get some repeat performances of success so we can keep the celebration going!

To keep success constant, we must discuss something else that needs consistency: Giving. (I know. Aren't we always giving something?) In addition to regularly giving a portion of your earnings to charity or some other cause that will benefit from your generosity, you must also be sure to maintain (or even ramp up!) your support for your man. You have to make sure you are being his personal cheerleader. A popular cheerleaders' cheer begins with "Gimme an A" and typically spells out a team name. The cheerleaders shout loudly and wave their pom-poms as they kick high and jump up and down for their team.

If you hadn't realized already, this book can help you become your man's best cheerleader. If he is already starting to earn money, keep that money train coming into your family's station by giving him constant words of encouragement. If he is still trying to make his first couple of sales, your words of encouragement are more important than ever. Having faith in him will make his success inevitable.

A Wise Woman's Words of Encouragement

I believe in you. I really admire your work ethic. Thank you for all you do for our family. I appreciate your hard work for our family. You are being an excellent example for our children. I'm so proud to be yours. You are my superstar. I love you.

Not only should you encourage your man, but you should also speak highly of your man and his efforts to work his network marketing business. This book is giving you strategies to help you deal with the time and effort it takes to build a network marketing business. However, you are probably not the only person who will feel the sting of your man's absence. Children, parents, in-laws, and friends will wonder why he is taking so much time away from his family to work on this new business. As a supportive mate, it is your job to keep up the morale amongst the ranks. If you have children, their father's absence from games, recitals, and the dinner table will be quite unsettling. This is especially true if he was always around before getting involved in the business. Your man should take the time to personally discuss what he is doing with your children. Together, they should schedule specific times when the children are guaranteed to see him.

Daddy's Reassuring Words

He may say something like, "Daddy is working on something right now that can make all of our lives better. It can help pay for some fun things you've always wanted and even pay for your college tuition down the road if all goes well. Sometimes, it's going to be tough on me and on you. I may not be able to make every game like I used to because of this new project. I may miss some family time. But I want you to know that I love you very much, and even when I'm not around, I'm always thinking about you."

Your man should also make sure the children have all of his telephone numbers so they can call him whenever they want to speak to him directly. He should encourage them to call him anytime. Making himself available by telephone will help alleviate some of the pain of his absence. The best promise your man can keep is the promise he makes to his children about when he will definitely be present for them. It may be in the morning before school, Sunday afternoons, or every day for a few hours after school. Whenever it is, this time should be non-negotiable. Spending scheduled time with the children will decrease the likelihood of them resenting the business for taking their father away from them. Children need love, too—as much as (and often even more than) you do!

Kevin, a top-producing network marketer and an equally impressive dad, makes a deal with his children that is worth sharing here. On the last day of each month, Kevin is mostly unavailable to his family. They know he is focused on following up with prospects and customers while making his final sales push to close the month out strong. In exchange for letting him work that day without interruptions, he gives them a special reward the next day. Sometimes it's a trip to the arcade; other times, they race cars at the go-cart track. Honestly, it really does not matter what the activity is. All that matters is that their dad is there and giving them his undivided attention. Although Kevin's children are not happy about sharing their dad with the business, having him all to themselves for hours of uninterrupted fun on the first day of every month is a date they look forward to with excited anticipation.

The attitudes of parents, in-laws, and friends regarding your man's time and business also need to be managed. At best, they may begin to question why he's never around. At worst, they may start to insinuate that he is having an affair. To prevent these conversations from affecting you, you must stop them before they start. You can do this by letting them know how excited you are about the business you both decided to join together, how proud you are that your man had the vision and courage to seize this opportunity, and how much you respect his work ethic and his progress in the business so far.

Note that I am not advocating making any earnings claims. Some people will be bold enough to ask you how much money you are making, but you would be wise not to talk about money for various reasons. What you want to convey is that you are completely supportive of your man's business and that you are working toward your family's goals as a couple.

Let me share with you what happened with Charles and Ramona. Charles was a hard-working network marketing man who loved his family. Ramona was raised by a single mother who had high hopes for her daughter to have the family life that eluded her—the devoted husband and happy children inside a loving home complete with a dog, all surrounded by a white picket fence living happily ever after.

Charles and Ramona jointly agreed to join a network marketing company. They both worked the business on a part-time, spare time basis. Because of their joint efforts, they began to have some success and receive a lot of recognition at the business meeting in their local area. Together, they thought, "Wow! If this is what we can generate part-time, what could happen if we *really* worked it?" They decided that Ramona would continue building the business part-time, but Charles would crank up his efforts in the business, while keeping his full-time job. This meant that when Charles was not at his job, he was out of the house working their business. Ramona was on-board and extremely supportive of this plan. Unfortunately, her mother was not.

Because Charles was often away, Ramona's mother began to wonder about his feelings toward her daughter and grandchildren. The good son-in-law and dedicated father she once knew was not around very much anymore. She believed it was just a matter of time before her daughter would be raising their children alone.

The resentment she felt for Charles grew stronger every day. When Ramona tried to explain that she supported Charles wholeheartedly and that Charles was working hard now so they could have more time as a family later, her explanations for Charles's absence fell on deaf ears. Ramona's mother felt that Ramona was being naïve to Charles's philandering ways. Whenever Ramona would ask her mother to help her with the children, her mother would say, "I'm busy. Where is your husband?"

Ramona's mother wanted Ramona to finally face what she believed was the demise of Ramona's marriage and leave Charles. If Ramona was going to eventually be a single mother, she may as well get on with it. Ramona felt very hurt and unsupported by her mother. Charles's desire to improve his family's financial situation had spawned a mother-in-law from hell.

Obviously, Ramona's mother's beliefs were far from the reality of the situation. The unfortunate truth of the matter is that her mother's attitude toward Charles did not improve until she started to see evidence of his work. Charles and Ramona bought new family room furniture and a flat-screen television to put above the fireplace. The children got a new computer. The icing on the cake was the weekend trip to the beach that Charles planned for everyone to enjoy—including Ramona's mother. After her mini-vacation, Ramona's mother began to soften her words about Charles with each passing day.

I told a good friend recently that, "Money is a naysayer slayer." The sad truth is that people need to be "shown the money" in order to shut-up. This goes for spouses, parents, in-laws, and friends. Sometimes, even you, too. No adult owes anybody any explanation, but results speak louder than words any day.

Will you be able to withstand the fiery words of others when they criticize you, your man, your business, and then question your sanity? I hope so. Network marketing requires you to do things that normal people wouldn't do, but it also allows you to have things that normal people don't have. More freedom. More time. More love. More money. Just to name a few.

When you are lonely and feeling blue about the business, never complain to people who do not understand network marketing. If you do, you will feel even worse than you were feeling before you started complaining to them. In tough times, I suggest getting your angst out by writing in a journal, talking to another network marketing wife or girlfriend (in your _upline_, not your downline), re-reading "The Best Advice" recommendations in Chapter 9, or going to the resources for the women of network marketing on my website at www. mlmwives.com/Guide.

Gimme a G-O T-E-A-M!

"If you want to be loved, be lovable."
- Ovid

Chapter 6

This Recruit is H-O-T

I'm going to be honest with you. Whether your man is spending most of his time building his business from home on the computer or running around town meeting people at Starbucks, Panera Bread, or in hotel lobbies, he will be encountering extremely attractive women who are either interested in or already involved in his network marketing business. People like to buy items from beautiful people. Some say that buying something from an attractive person makes purchasers feel better about themselves. Whatever the reason, good-looking people are easy on the eye and increase the chances of us paying attention to sales pitches. Hence, companies pay large sums of money for models to sell products on television and in magazines.

The business of network marketing is selling products and services. I can guarantee you there will be an above-average number of beautiful women who are involved in the business with your man. I am not saying this to intimidate you or to cause you to question your man's ability to remain faithful. I am just preparing you. When you know what you are dealing with in advance, you can plan ahead.

Plan to attend business meetings and events with your man. It will be good for the business and for your relationship. Your man will appreciate your support and your being by his side, and you both will be learning more about the business together. In addition, all of his colleagues will meet you. This is very important. People in network marketing know that people who have complete support from home have a far greater chance of success in the business than those who don't. Your presence also serves notice to some of the more unscrupulous women in the room that your man is not such an easy target.

Attractive or not, women who actively work their own network marketing businesses are typically not daunted by rejection. They deal with "no" regularly as they build their businesses. As a result, they are not fearful of propositioning a man and being rejected. It's more like a challenge to them. It would be naïve for you to believe that some flirty business floozy wouldn't try to make a seductive move on your man. If you think your man is attractive, chances are, someone else does, too.

If your man experiences success and becomes a rising superstar, he will get even more attention. There will be increased interest in him for legitimate business reasons and maybe some "not-so-legitimate" reasons among women in the business. Women are drawn to power and money like a magnet. I'm sure you have seen some very strange pairings of rich men with beautiful young *tenderonis* on their arms. Remember Anna Nicole Smith and her billionaire husband J.

Howard Marshall II? When they married, she was 26 and he was 89. What about Hugh Hefner and the young hotties who live with him at his Playboy mansion? Seeing them together makes you think, "They are only with him for his money." I won't even mention the names of the numerous professional athletes who have been caught in adulterous relationships with groupies. The point I am trying to make is this: stuff happens. While you can't eliminate the chances entirely, you can do your part to make sure this scandalous stuff doesn't happen to you.

Often, in a marriage or even in a long-term relationship, people get comfortable. Those high heels you wore when you were trying to win him over are buried deep in the closet, replaced by more comfortable flats that don't hurt your feet. That long hair you used to toss ever-so-coyly during dinner by candlelight before you agreed to a committed relationship is now in a scrunchie more often than falling loosely at your shoulders. That little nightie is in the back of your drawer because all you wear to bed now are big t-shirts, flannel pajama pants, and socks. Stop. It. Now. Don't do it. Give yourself a fighting chance against those ambitiously sly women. Entice your man to keep a picture in his head of you and your sexy instead of fantasizing about another woman's sexy. I know this is tough to hear, but I would be remiss if I was not honest with you about some of the women in the business.

Besides physical attraction, your man could be tempted by his emotions. Building a network marketing business is a learning experience. People learn a lot about themselves and others as they encounter various personalities. Through motivational materials and business experiences, your man will be growing and changing. At the same time, as a couple, you will either be growing closer together or further apart. If you are reading the same books, listening to the same CDs, and experiencing the journey of building a network marketing business with him, you will be growing closer together as a couple. On the other hand, if you refuse to attend meetings and conferences, constantly mock his efforts, and have nothing good to say about anything related to the business, you will be growing apart. He will want to spend more time with like-minded people who will listen to him and sympathize with his experiences. Most men have a low threshold of patience for listening, but a woman who has designs on your man will give him her attentive ear for as long as he needs it. Before you know it, your man could be the poster child for emotional infidelity. And where the road of emotional infidelity ends, adultery often begins. This is yet another reason to get on board the business bandwagon. It may not be your *"thing,"* but because it is his *"thing,"* get interested and stay interested. Experiencing personal growth and mindset changes together will maintain and strengthen your relationship.

Despite the cautionary words above, there will be women whom he recruits in the business that he must work with closely. It will be platonic. There will be other women who are not is his downline or upline that he may work with on the telephone or in person from time to time. It will also be platonic. I am not suggesting that your man will have a wandering eye or a wandering anything else that may cause him to stray away from home. My message to you is to stay alert. Keep yourself attractive and pulled together nicely. Don't greet him at the end of the workday with an appearance that screams your workday was worse than his. Be easy on his eyes when he comes home from work. Attend events with him (looking your absolute best, of course), and continually discuss with one another the impact the business is having on your lives individually and as a couple. Above all, trust your man.

More than any pair of stilettos or barely-there Victoria Secret negligee, your unconditional support of his business and his dreams are the ultimate in sexy. A man cannot flourish without the respect and admiration of his lady. Doubting his ideas and questioning his abilities will eventually drive him away. Instead of trying to criticize and control him, focus on controlling *yourself* and *your* criticism. When your man feels your support and adoration, he'll always remember that his hottest recruit is at home. Wink. Wink.

"Love is not measured in moments of time,
but in timeless moments."
- Anonymous

Chapter 7

This Relationship is H-O-T-T-E-R

*Y*our man will be pulled in many directions. He may be working his full-time job during the day, working his network marketing business in the evening, and keeping the time commitments he made to the children. By the time he comes home to you he is exhausted. He prefers to decompress from his day by listening to the talking heads on ESPN rather than listening to the latest details of what is happening with you. Over time, this loss of companionship can lead to frustration and anger. It can cause you to resent your man and the business. This loss of connection causes emotional detachment from each other, which is very unhealthy for your relationship.

To keep your relationship HOT amidst everything else going on in your lives, you both have to make spending quality time together a priority. Don't let too much time pass between date nights with each other. Your man will be meeting potential recruits to discuss the business primarily during evenings, lunch times, and weekends. These are the times most people are enjoying time with their families or pursuing personal interests and hobbies.

Although network marketing requires a huge time commitment, everyone makes time for what they feel is important no matter how busy they are. As his personal Very Important Person (VIP), you deserve to have a recurring entry in his calendar of appointments. The tricky part is learning to be flexible about it.

The nature of the business requires that you remain open to being spontaneous. Savvy network marketers strike when the prospect is hot and ready, because once prospects cool down, they may never be interested again. Understanding this, you can make plans loosely with *"open scheduling."* Rather than being steadfast on a specific day and time, you and your man can agree to do a specific activity together during the week, while leaving the day and time for the activity open and flexible. For example, you can agree to meet for lunch one day this week, without specifying the day or time. The great thing about open scheduling is that he has five days to make it happen, and you reduce your chances of disappointment. He has more time to see how his schedule for the week is coming together. This relieves some of the pressure from both of you. When you don't specify a day or time, your feelings aren't hurt when he has to cancel and reschedule for business reasons. Also, if your schedule is filling up and the day you initially chose is not ideal, you can reschedule to a day that works better for you. You can still look forward to the lunch knowing that it'll happen another day in the week as agreed. With open scheduling, by the end of the week, you'll have lunch when both of you are available, relaxed, and totally focused on enjoying time together.

Going with the flow usually allows for more time together, rather than less. In addition to time you plan to spend together, there may also be time for spontaneous rendezvous. When you are flexible and willing to work with his changing schedule, you'll make him want to spend his downtime with you. He will know he can relax with you, instead of having to guard himself from being pounced on with nags and complaints. Your man will look forward to seeing you and will call you if his appointments cancel or his meetings get moved. Making it easy on him actually makes it better for you.

Once you finally get him physically present for your quality couple time, you must require that he give you the same undivided attention and respect as he would a H-O-T prospect—after all, you are H-O-T aren't you? (If not, reread Chapter 6.) He must be ready to be completely engaged and totally present with you. Distractions must be eliminated. This includes cell phones, computers, televisions, and children. In return for your patience and flexibility, his complete attention and focus on you when you are together is the least he can do. Don't compromise on this point. Set your standard and don't budge. Make sure he respects your time as he would a prospect's time. After all, you are more important than any prospect. You are his VIP.

To enhance their quality time experiences together, my friend Don gives his cell phone to his wife Elaina when they have a date night. This small gesture gets big points for assuring Elaina that she is more important than his business. With his cell phone in her purse, Elaina also knows she has Don's undivided attention for the evening, especially if she happens to question his priorities at any other time.

Quality time arrangements vary from individual to individual, but I generally recommend you make an appointment for a date with your man no less than twice per month—more if possible, and he should accommodate. An easy way to squeeze quality couple time into two busy lives is to set your alarm clock an hour earlier to exercise together in the morning before the demands of the day officially start. As you know, exercise increases your energy, makes you feel better, and reduces stress. Having a fit and toned physique is attractive, so why not work out together? The couple that works out together, can work everything out. Try it.

If mornings are a challenge for you, another way to have quality couple time is for your man to bring home a late dinner to share when he comes in after a long day of work and meetings. Or, after you prepare dinner, you can feed the children and put them to bed, and wait to eat dinner with your man when he comes home later. This will enable you to share the day's highlights with one another and have a relaxing conversation together. Eating late will not be great for your waistlines, but it can keep the flames of love burning in two busy lives.

To support your efforts to keep your relationship H-O-T, I have created two pledges—one for each of you to sign. These pledges will remind both of you to be considerate of one another, and your relationship, while building the network marketing business. You can download your free copy of "My Presence Pledge" and "My Patience Pledge" at www.mlmwives.com/Guide.

"The only thing worse than a man you can't control is a man you can."
- Margo Kaufman

Chapter 8

Bossy Babes Beware

*a*s I am sure you know by now, building a network marketing business can be tough on a marriage. Building the business takes a lot of his time and attention, which is time and attention away from you. This often leaves you feeling lonely, unappreciated, and unsupported. You feel emotionally drained. How can you be expected to give love, support, and attention to your man whenever he needs it when he rarely gives it to you? This is a common source of friction.

Remember the Law of Reciprocity? Give and receive? Because of the business, you are usually giving more than receiving, which, if left imbalanced for too long, can cause irreparable harm to your relationship.

Every woman has a limit. There is a certain point when you will feel like you can't take it anymore. You will not be cancelled on another time. You will not be late to another event because you are waiting on him to finish a business meeting. You will not explain to the children again why their father cannot be at the game. You will not lie in bed alone another night while he works on the computer. You will no longer tolerate having your conversation interrupted by a telephone call that he has to take because of "the business." That's it. You will not give any more of yourself without getting the time, love, and attention you need in return.

I understand how you feel. Your feelings are completely reasonable. A self-respecting woman can only sacrifice so much. If money is not an issue either because you have your own money or because your man is making money in the business (or both), this breaking point takes longer to reach. If the money is funny, honey, you will run out of patience with the business rather quickly.

You will know when you have reached your breaking point. It is the point when your patience has been worn so thin that you feel that you and your man's business cannot coexist in his life. You will feel an urgent need to have a serious conversation with your man to give him the ultimate **ultimatum**. You will tell him he must make a choice: you or "the business."

Hopefully, you are reading this book before you have reached your breaking point. If so, perfect. This book can be a warning of what can potentially happen if you don't employ some of the suggestions discussed in this book. Or, you may have already been fed up with the business and are reading this book in an attempt to have a better understanding of the force that has overcome your man, who used to be so attentive and available. That's fine, too. Whoever you are, wherever you are, let me offer some words of guidance.

Ultimatums are never good. Making your man choose between you and his business will produce an outcome destined for disaster. If he chooses you, he will resent the fact that you backed him into a corner and forced him to quit the business. Whenever a financial crisis arises, he'll use it as an opportunity to remind you that he had a business that could have provided financial stability. That is, until you made him quit. You do not want to be blamed for his failure to fulfill his dream for the rest of your life, nor do you want to look back and wonder where you both might be if the business really worked out in the long run.

On the other hand, what if your man feels so strongly about the business and where he's going with it, that he surprises you with his answer to your ultimatum. He picks the business. Yikes! He feels you have been so unsupportive of his goals and dreams that he will be better off without all of your negativity and nagging about the time, love, and attention you need. Ouch. Perhaps you should have approached him in a different way. Yes, you should have.

Instead of ultimatums, conversations about compromises work better. Compromise is about giving something and receiving something. Sound familiar? In a compromise, both people may not get *all* of what they want, but both people get *some* of what they want and are generally much happier with the outcome than with the "all or nothing" result an ultimatum demands. Whether you have already given your man an ultimatum or not, a conversation about compromise is the way to get more of what you want.

Conversations About Compromise

Having a conversation about compromise may happen like this: "I see how serious you are about your business, and I respect your dedication and work ethic. But I am feeling (lonely, upset, angry, sad—insert whatever adjective you feel is appropriate here). I miss the time we used to spend together. Do you think there is a way we can be together more that still allows you the time you need to work your business? I really miss (being with you/having you at the dinner table/being together as a family—insert whatever you really miss)."

This approach is not nagging, argumentative, or bossy. You are not telling him he must choose. You are simply sharing your feelings with him, showing him you respect his business, but also letting him know that you miss him. I can't imagine a man who would not be agreeable to finding more time to do whatever it is he needs to do to make the supportive woman he loves happy. When you approach him with love, he will respond with love. Once again, give and receive.

So that you are not always waiting around, watching clocks and keeping track of the time your man is not around, you must find ways to occupy your time that are interesting enough to you to keep yourself busy. Network marketing business aside, it is healthier for your relationship for you to have a life outside of your relationship. Often, women get so caught up with life as a couple that they forget they had their own life before a man showed up. Women lose touch with close girlfriends and even stop connecting with family members, making their man their everything. It is not healthy to fall into this trap.

Get your own life! Rediscover yourself! Enjoy your own company!

Finding ways to enjoy your leisure time separate and apart from your relationship is really not that difficult. Focus on pursuing hobbies and interests that you have always wanted to explore. Join a women's group or book club that has regular meetings and activities. Reach out to other women who are in relationships with men involved in the business. Take a class. Volunteer. Learn something new. Exercise. You can even become more involved in your man's network marketing business, or alternatively, start your *own* business! Find something to do that brings you happiness and satisfaction. If you are busy doing something you enjoy, you won't be as apt to scream at your man for being so busy with his business.

I have one final point about being bossy to share with you. Do you appreciate it when people try to tell you how to do something when they haven't even done it themselves? In other words, their advice is pure theory supported by no real experience, yet they think they are giving you an expert opinion. This happens often with people who don't have children but who feel the need to tell parents how they should raise their kids. It also happens with teenagers who haven't lived long enough to know much about life, but want to argue with their parents about how life is. This can also happen with a well-intentioned woman who is genuinely trying to help her man in a business, but knows nothing of what she speaks because she has not had the training and experience with the business that her man has had thus far. Does this sound like you, Ms. Lady?

Even though your intention is to be supportive, don't try to tell your man how to run the business, especially if you aren't actively involved in it. Even if you *are* actively working the business, don't speak to your man like you are his boss. You can strategize with him, confer with him, problem-solve together, but don't tell him what to do. His goal is to fire his boss and be a full-time entrepreneur. He is certainly not working hard to be bossed around in his own home.

Ban your inner "Bossy Babe" and unleash your unconditional support with vengeance. Your man will feel very fortunate to have you in his life. In gratitude, he will want to give you all the love and attention you desire—and so much more!

"When you are willing to sacrifice everything, you don't really have to. God works everything out."
- Chanelle Burt

Chapter 9

The Best Advice

*W*ithout a doubt, you now know that your support is extremely vital to your man's success. Your support, coupled with his work ethic, could result in achieving major personal and financial satisfaction in the network marketing business. This book has demonstrated that "his business is your business."

When you work as a team, you both win. When you are supportive of the business, he will want to give you everything you desire, including lots of love, time, and attention. This mutual cycle of love and support and support and love will continue as long as you both make regular contributions to it.

Life won't be perfect, but if you both do the things today that others won't do, so that tomorrow, you have the freedom and lifestyle that others don't have, life will be perfect enough. Trust me.

My mentors in the network marketing business teach that our priorities should be ordered this way: God first, family second, and business third. As your man gets busier in the business, you may feel that his priorities are all wrong. Clearly, at some point, it may seem that the business has become more important to him than his family, and maybe even his spirituality. I've actually heard concerned family members and friends suggest that network marketing businesses are cults. The truth of the matter is all of his work is for his family. This seems ironic because he's absent so much that the family is wondering if he still loves them more than he loves the business.

The reality is that many of us have never seen what true sacrifice and commitment looks like. Very few people work their jobs so intensely that they have to explain their superhuman work ethic to their loved ones. That kind of commitment is not required on a regular job. Rightly so. Jobs don't pay people enough to make the sacrifices that success in network marketing requires. This is why the reward from a network marketing business can be so huge. It's also why many people don't stick around for the long haul. The price of success is so expensive that most people aren't willing to pay it. When the average person is confronted with decisions that involve personal sacrifice—such as loss of time with loved ones, loss of friends with whom they can no longer relate, and loss of significant others who do not support them—their lack of conviction will cause them to turn back towards the familiar and away from personal growth, which is a requirement for long-term success. Only those with a strong mind and tenacious heart will have massive success in network marketing. You can garner the strength necessary to win in network marketing very easily when you make your WHY big enough.

I believe that beside every good man is a strong woman. I also believe women who share knowledge share strength. The best advice I can give you, besides everything else I have already shared in this book, is to get comfortable with being uncomfortable and enjoy the ride. Nothing worth having comes easy. If success was easy, everyone would have it.

Please visit my website at www.mlmwives.com to stay in touch and get resources to support you on your journey through network marketing. If you have any questions about the topics covered in this book or the network marketing business in general, please do not hesitate to email me. I welcome your opinions and comments.

Remember to visit my website to download your free copy of the "My Presence Promise" pledge and the "My Patience Promise" pledge. You will also find updates and information on upcoming events, speaking engagements, and training programs.

I wish you the absolute best in life, in love, and in business. Here's to you and your man's success in network marketing. Cheers!

Email your questions and comments to
Angela@mlmwives.com

Follow me on Twitter
@AngelaGSolomon and @MLMWives

Like my FB Page www.facebook.com/AngelaGSolomon
to receive all of my updates.

ACKNOWLEDGMENTS

*W*ow! What an amazing and exciting journey this has been. Writing my first book (and self-publishing it!) has been quite a learning experience. Of course, I didn't do it alone. A team of people helped me to get this book project to the finish line. Here are the people to whom I am grateful:

Orin Solomon, my superhero husband, whose unconditional love and total support of me writing this book made all the difference in the world.

Ollie Goodlow, my mother, whose determination to reach her goals rubbed off on me in a good way.

Alvin Goodlow, Jr., my dad, with whom my children stayed for three weeks, which allowed me to concentrate on getting the words out of my head to complete this book.

The 3 J's, my children, who watched this book "grow up" and always understood when I needed quiet time for "the Book."

Mildred Johnson and Marvaline Muirhead, my grandmother and great-aunt, because it doesn't seem right to acknowledge a bunch of other people without showing them some love, too.

Karen Liverman, Alecia Goodlow-Young, Berlin Onumonu, and Makila Bey, who all took time to give their advice on the project whenever I asked.

Shawn Mason Spence, my co-Mastermind Mommy, whose ideas and encouragement without a doubt caused this book to be born after years of sitting idle on an old computer hard-drive.

Robert G. Allen, whose inspiring words motivated me to complete this book. I am extremely grateful for your generous endorsement.

Diane Kennedy, CPA extraordinaire, I remember your enthusiastic willingness to help me when I told you about this book. Thank you for taking the time to write the foreword.

Sharman Monroe, my first reader and editor, whose on-point feedback made this a better book.

Lisa Abbate, my editor, whose guidance, knowledge, and encouragement kept me focused on the finish and made this a better book.

Jeniffer Thompson, Anna Bobro, Julio Pompa, and Stephanee Killen, who all shared their talents with me so that I could showcase mine.

To every family member, teacher, and friend who ever told me, "You're a great writer." This book is for you.

NETWORK MARKETING AND ME (AND HIM, TOO!)

I was born and raised in Detroit, Michigan. My parents taught me to go to school and get good grades so that I could get a good job. Graduating from college was not an option. It was a requirement.

After getting an undergraduate business degree, I landed my first job as a Financial Analyst for a Fortune 100 company that paid me an annual salary of $30,000. I felt very proud of myself (and my parents were proud, too). I was independent and self-sufficient. I paid rent for my own downtown, high-rise apartment; I bought my own little red sports car; and I moved to Minneapolis, Minnesota where I didn't know a soul before my first day of work. I was living the dream of a successful, all-grown-up college graduate.

On my way to climbing the corporate ladder of success, I worked diligently and built an excellent professional rapport with my colleagues. I was promoted from Financial Analyst to Business Analyst relatively quickly. By my third year of employment, I was participating in strategic planning meetings with the company's top executives. One of my responsibilities was the weekly preparation of a very high-profile sales report that was distributed to all of the company's offices around the country. My goal was to become the youngest Vice President in the company. I was on the fast track, just as I had planned.

A telephone call I received one day changed my career path forever. A friend invited me to a network marketing opportunity meeting. After weeks of making excuses about why I could not attend, I decided to go to the meeting. My sole purpose for going to the meeting was to poke holes in whatever gimmick my friend was peddling.

To my surprise, the concept presented at the meeting made perfect sense to me. Who wouldn't want to earn passive, residual income working for themselves? Upon being introduced to the presenter, I contained my excitement about the business opportunity because as well as I was doing on my job, I didn't have $500 to spare for the start-up fee.

Fortunately, I was able to capitalize on another opportunity presented at the meeting. The speaker that evening eventually became my husband. As fate would have it, he was in Minneapolis to present the opportunity on the evening I decided to attend.

Not long thereafter, the three of us became inseparable—my husband, me, and network marketing.

Being exposed to entrepreneurship through network marketing exposed me to a different way to achieve my professional goals and help a lot of people along the way. I realized that working for myself could be as professionally rewarding as climbing the corporate ladder—and a lot more fun! I quickly used up the ten vacation days I was allotted from my job as I traveled around the country building the network marketing business with my then fiancé. Working closely with him made me realize that our combined talents and efforts could lead us to unbelievable success. I made a bold but brilliant decision to quit my job and move to Washington, DC to be with my partner in business and in love.

Of course, the words of my mother were never far from my mind. She emphatically taught me to always be able to take care of myself, with or without a husband. So when I said, "I do," I had already completed my first year of law school. When I walked across the stage to receive my law degree, I was expecting our first child.

Thanks to my husband's super-human work ethic, our network marketing business was going extremely well. After passing the bar exam, I was anxious to put my law degree to work. I was happy practicing business and corporate law, but I was coming home from work mentally exhausted. I enjoyed the work and my clients, but I felt that I was not giving my best effort to my most important client—my son.

The value of network marketing became very apparent to me when I announced to my husband that I would be quitting my job to be a full-time mother to our son. Upon hearing my news, my husband didn't flinch. He gave me a very support-ive, "Okay" and didn't miss a beat. For me, network market-ing means freedom to make choices to live the lifestyle you desire. This is quite a contrast from my corporate life, where freedom and choices were not highlights of the employee benefits package.

The prediction I made years before was correct: We are an awesome team! I am still as ambitious and independent as I was when I met him. He is my superhero, and I am his trusty, supportive companion. We each bring our individual strengths and talents to our life and business partnership. We use our combined efforts to help as many people as possible benefit from all that network marketing has to offer.

Total support from home is a key component to success in network marketing. I wrote *The Ultimate Guide for the Network Marketer's Bride* to help more couples get involved in network marketing using a team approach to increase their likelihood of success. I believe that beside every great man is a spectacular woman. Together, you can do extraordinary things for yourselves and so many others.

So what are you waiting for? Get the love you desire and build an empire! I'll see you at the top!

Wishing you enormous success in life, love, and business,

Angela

ABOUT THE AUTHOR

*P*rior to network marketing, Angela G. Solomon graduated from the University of Michigan - Ann Arbor with a Bachelor of Business Administration. After working in corporate America for three years, she returned to the George Washington University National Law Center, where she earned a law degree.

Angela has over fourteen years of experience as a wife and network marketer. Network marketing allowed Angela to retire from the practice of law and concentrate her efforts on raising her family and building a business with her husband. One of Angela's passions is helping women succeed in business and in relationships. Her other passions include spending time with her husband and her three sons, traveling the world, and reading novels.

Born in Detroit, Michigan, Angela now resides in the Washington, D.C. area with her family.